LEADERSHIP

Followers, Behaviors, Tools

A Practical Guide for Leaders

C. Ray Collins

LEADERSHIP

Quantity sales special discounts are available on quantity purchases by corporations, associations, and others. For details, contact the publisher at the address above.

Orders by U.S. trade bookstores and wholesalers. Email info@ BeyondPublishing.net

The Beyond Publishing Speakers Bureau can bring authors to your live event. For more information or to book an event contact the Beyond Publishing Speakers Bureau speak@BeyondPublishing.net

Author can be reached directly at claudec53@hotmail.com

Manufactured and printed in the United States of America distributed globally by BeyondPublishing.net

BEYOND

New York | Los Angeles | London | Sydney

ISBN Hardcover: 978-1-947256-31-6

FOREWORD

When I decided to write this book, I had already written a fiction book and thought this book would be easier to write. Well, I was very wrong. Writing a non-fiction book is different than writing a fiction book.

With the fiction book, you can change an event or time or place to make it all work out in your story. But, with nonfiction book, you can't do that. You have to stay with the facts, the research, and the truth. Try to deliver it so people can understand and use what you write.

Leadership is probably one of the most written about subjects. That is because it is needed in almost every activity you do. Whether playing games, being a member of a club, in every work force, every business, etc. There are always common contents, such as different styles of leadership. Different types of situations. How to decide which style is right for you in every book you read.

With my book, I'm going to take you into the practical use. Tell you why the leader and follower program work. I'm going to give you tools to use to help you be the leader that people will want to follow and work for. I will help you develop your follower abilities and get the most from them.

I will address different behaviors and habits that will benefit you, as a leader.

Leaders, Followers, Behavior, and Tools will lead you to be a better leader, if not a great leader.

C. Ray Collins

INTRODUCTION

I have been in some type of management / supervisory role for 40 years. I'm also a student of two experts in leadership / communication art:

Dale Carnegie, *The Quick & Easy Way to Effective Speaking* and *How to Win Friends and Influence People*

Nicholas Boothman, *Convince Them in 90 Seconds or Less* and *The Irresistible Power of Story Speak*

I attended four different colleges / universities: Floyd Junior College in Roman, Georgia, Louisiana State University in Shreveport, Louisiana, East Central University, in Ada, Oklahoma, and Texas A&M in College Station, Texas toward a business degree. I'm also an author of a fiction book, *What If It Were Possible,* a sci-fi novel.

Nothing here makes me "special" compared to others who have books out on leadership.

What makes me different is I started my career in the construction industry as a field laborer. After few short months, I moved into a trade and soon became a journeyman. A few years later, I became a supervisor. Supervising crews from three or four people to several crews of 30 and 40 people.

I continued to work hard, continued my education, and before long, I moved into the management role of departments and later managing projects worth hundreds of million dollars or more. Which included managing a direct staff of 50 to 100 people and 30 to 40 contractors all at one time.

So, I understand what it is to be the follower as in the worker, follower and leader as in mid-management, and also the leader, as in the "buck stops here". With this, I can give an insight that others can't give you. Let's get started!

CONTENT

CHAPTER 1

LEADERS

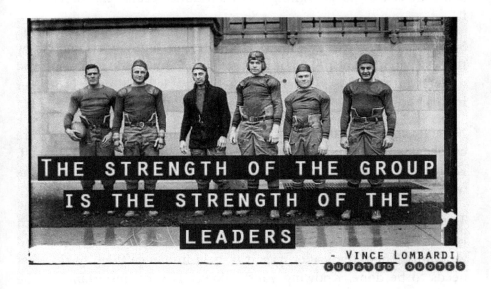

THE STRENGTH OF THE GROUP
IS THE STRENGTH OF THE
LEADERS

- VINCE LOMBARDI
CURATED QUOTES

Before we get into what I think is more important and beneficial to you, we need to cover the basics of leadership. The first few chapters will probably be boring to most of you, because I will be covering things you have heard or read before. But it needs to be said.

Wikipedia says a leader: "Is one who influences or leads others". In other words, you are giving them direction and guidance to do what you want done in a way they want to do it, not just for you, but for themselves.

It also says that leadership is: "A process of social influence in which one or more persons attempts to enlist the aid and support of others in accomplishment of task or tasks."

This can be interpreted in different ways.

Dale Carnegie says of leadership: "There only one way to get people to do anything, just one way. That's by influencing others in a way that they want to do it."

President Dwight Eisenhower said, "Leadership is the art of getting someone else to do something you want done because he wants to do it."

So, what these two are saying is that you must influence someone by the way you interact and communicate with them. To do this, you must understand some human behaviors, which we will get into a little later in this book.

Now, **Randy Stocklin**, CEO of OneClick Ventures says: "Leaders are coaches, with the passion for developing people, not players." And **J. Kelly Huey**, author of *Build your Dream Team*, says leaders are "someone who builds their team, mentors them, and then advocates for them".

These two leaders look at developing people and building a team, which is also a part of leadership that considers the follower's strengths and weakness. Then, the leader uses it to help influence them to do what needs to be done. Knowing your follower is very important for the leader/ follower relationship.

Nicholas Boothman says: "Great leaders use storytelling to change attitudes and behaviors, rally, and inspire followers since the beginning of time."

So, what we see here, is several factors can play a role in being a good leader. Just being experienced in the business and knowing the direction to go isn't enough to lead your follower to a good end-result.

You need to understand and use:

- Human behaviors
- Communication skills
- Knowing your followers
- Follower's strengths
- Follower's weaknesses

But this is just some of what important to be a good leader. You are thinking that you understand this, and some of you probably do. But the question is, do you know how to put this to practical use?

As we continue on, you are going to learn how to use these things and others in your day-to-day operation. Being a leader is a full-time job. Surprisingly, being a good leader is also part of our natural abilities, as you will learn. Great leadership takes full advantage of natural abilities, behaviors, and common ground to accomplish the task at hand.

We will learn how our natural abilities and behaviors play a large role in the leader and follower's relationship.

Knowing your follower and relying on their natural abilities and behavior is going to play an important role to all your success.

CHAPTER 2

STYLES

Every book on leadership addresses different styles of leadership, ranging from four to six different styles.

Styles are important to know they exist. Sometimes, it's hard to know which style you are or the one you using, because in a lot of cases, we use all of them at some point and time. A good leader changes styles, depending on the follower. As with leaders, there are different type of followers.

In "Firewalkers Guide to Leadership", Tony Robbins says there are six different styles of leaders. You can be one of these or a combination of all of these.

- **Democratic**
- **Visionary**
- **Coaching**
- **Affiliative**
- **Pacesetting**
- **Commanding**

Tony's styles are probably the better-known ones. Here are the definitions:

Democratic: Places high value on diverse skills, qualities, and knowledge base of a team. Examples: politicians, senators, and can apply to corporate presidents. (To me, this type other leader, in many cases, fails. That is because they rely totally on others. Sometimes, they don't have enough knowledge or experience with the subject to be a good leader.)

Visionary: Ability to come up with new directions and new potential solutions to a problem. Thinking outside the box. Example: Steve Jobs/ Apple. (This person can usually be a motivator. Even thinking outside the box, the direction/ solution must be achievable and realistic.)

Coaching: One who spends time and energy on individuals in any given group. They will direct, guide, and cultivate others based on what influences their desires in a positive way. Example: project managers, sport coaches. (You will find these leaders can be somewhat emotional in their leadership style.)

Affiliative: Places high emphasis on the "team". Building trust within a group and creating an emotional bond. A sense of belonging. Praise and encouragement are important. Example: football coaches, teachers, and ministers. (This only works in business if it is in combination with another style.)

Pacesetting: Leads by example. They set and live by high standards and hope others will follow. Example: drill sergeant, minister, and other leader styles. (I think leaders, in general, are pacesetters.)

Commanding: "Do as I say because I'm the boss" attitude. Gives directives and expects other to follow. Example: military officers, stage directors. (At times, all leaders must become the commanding leader.)

Throughout my career, I have used all of these. Sometimes, two or three at the same time. Your behavior is based on your follower's behavior. You may switch back and forth to different styles, depending on the follower, circumstances, and desired outcome.

It is a little hard to choose. I like to think I'm more of the Democratic and Affiliative most of the time, but I know other styles fits me as well.

You have your own style, whether it's one of these or not. It's all about how you relate to your followers in a positive way to get the job done.

I wanted to give this information to you. It's important to know this, but it more important to know how to use it. You will see how all this comes into play as we get into behaviors and habits.

Think for a minute, which style are you? It could be two or three styles. To me, it would be hard to use the Coaching style without the Democratic style.

Going back to the definition of leader/ leadership. You must remember you are the **influencer** or the **controller**. Yes, I used the word controller or **manipulator**, you are wanting to control or manipulate your follower's actions to accomplish tasks in the best possible way. These are not bad words. It why some people refer to others as a "control freak". But good leaders use them in a positive way. You are controlling people actions. Yes, it's true.

The followers are the ones who have the "**Desire to help or the want to**" behavior. They don't only want to help you, but they want to please you. Having this behavior, they also want to do it for themselves. For some, this is their chosen role. For others, it the stepping stone to learn more, become more, and perhaps become a leader themselves one day.

With the leader having the influencer / controller behavior and the follower having the desire to help or want to behavior, it's easy to see why the leader / follower relationship works.

The boss (the leader) and the worker (the follower) relationship are the same. But just a note, you don't have to be the boss to be a leader. Every department, every crew, has leaders within a group that leads and mentors the others.

That because everyone has certain inherent abilities or behaviors we are born with. It's part of your natural behavior.

As we move forward, you will see that the leader and the follower have similar inherent and learned abilities and behaviors. These similarities are necessary to have a relationship between leader and follower.

CHAPTER 3

ABILITIES AND BEHAVIORS

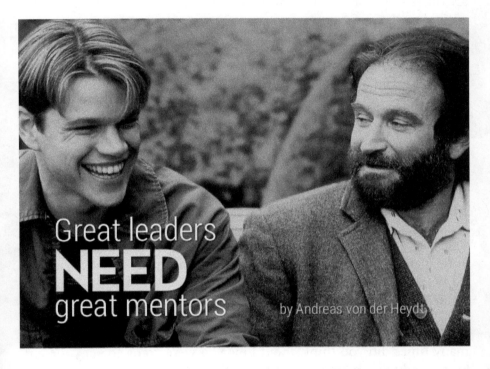

Great leaders **NEED** great mentors   by Andreas von der Heydt

I mention that the leader's and the follower's abilities / behaviors are inherent. What if I told you, everyone has both abilities / behaviors? Yes, they do.

I know some of you are thinking to yourself, *I don't have any leadership abilities.* Well, let me show you that you do.

Researchers from Harvard, New York University, and University of California conduit research working with 1,000 participants discovered a genetic trait, which they were able to correlate directly with leadership abilities. This research also shows several genetic traits that correlated with leadership: honesty, creativity, and teaching. They also found submissive, loyalty, supportive, and acceptance traits, which are good for followers.

However, all these are found in ALL the participants.

This is just a few of their results, but enough to prove my point. There are other ways for you to know this. Inherent is like the baby knows to suck a nipple for food.

Remember these are abilities and behaviors. Not to confuse them with natural body reactions, such as breathing, or something inherited from you parents, such as eye color.

If you can, remember back when you were a child. How many times did you try to influence your parents in letting you do something you want to do? Maybe you try to convince them that you were old enough to go and do something? Even before then, when you were a small baby, you did this without learning—if you cried, you got their attention, or when you wanted to be fed or held, you would cry. That was you having influence over you parents or manipulating them.

How many times did you plan and act on your plan to get a friend to do what you wanted? Several, I'm sure. So, we start early. Planning, influencing, manipulating, and taking control.

Let's go a little further, how about when you started dating? How many times did you think about how you were going to get your girl/boy friend to do what you wanted? Whether it was to see a movie you wanted to see, or maybe a dance you wanted to go to, you were taking control, being the influencer, being manipulative. You were trying to be the leader.

I also said you had the inherent ability / behavior to be a follower. Do you agree? Let's look at this the same way as the leader.

How many times do you remember saying to your parents when you were a young child, "Let me help"? You did this as young as when you first started talking. Maybe you also said, "Let me, I can do this."

Sometimes, you would do something you knew they wanted done. Just so you could show them you could do it. You wanted to make them happy, you wanted to help. You wanted to do what they wanted done. Not just for them, but for yourself. This is the follower behavior.

Even in school, you have a teacher who you want to please or even help out where you could. That's the follower in you, and that particular teacher was a leader influencing you.

As you grew and more interactive, you developed or learned other behaviors. With these added behaviors, you let one or the other—leader or follower—dominate you.

Since we possess both, then it would be natural for the leader and the follower to have a lot in common. Let's compare the leader and follower:

LEADERS	FOLLOWERS
Communicator	Communicator
Motivator	Motivator
Decision Maker	Loyal
Inspirer	Desire to Help
Coach	Coachable
Invested	Invested
Team Player	To Belong
Negotiator	Supporter
Expert	Expert
Model	Model
Fact Finder	Fact Finders

LEADERS	FOLLOWERS
Influencer	Submissive
Controller	A Doer
Problem Solver	Creative
Manipulator	The Want to
Teacher	Student
Honest	Loyal
Mentor	

These similarities are necessary to have the relationship between leader and follower.

We talked about the different leaders, now we need to cover the different types of followers. Some authors have broken this down into to several types. But to me, I think you can simplify these down. There are only three different types.

- **Loyalist**
- **Achiever**
- **Reserved**

The Loyalist is the follower who follows you because you are a good leader and will do whatever is asked of them. They are self-motivated, and they are loyal and will always work to make you look good. You can always rely on them to follow through with their assignments. They are good team members and support all of the team. They become your rock. Your go-to people, and they will always be followers. If you are lucky, some of these will be highly skilled or experts at what they do. They are also willing to show others on the team.

The Achiever has all the qualities of your loyalist, but they are wanting more. They are highly motived and eager to learn. They follow you not just because you are a good leader, but also because you are fair, and a good teacher / mentor. These are the ones who are usually the leaders within your team. Sometimes, you will promote them to what some call leadmen or assistant. They really don't require added attention; they just need opportunities to use their abilities, have more challenges, and hone their communication skills. Some of these will continue their path to become leaders of their own team/crew in the future. Some of these are open about their ambitions, and others aren't. That's why it important to know your followers. Learn what their abilities, their strengths, and their weaknesses are. Know their behaviors. You learn what motivates them.

The Reserved is a follower who a little different than the other two. Now, they can have the same qualities as the Loyalist without the motivation—they follow you, not only because you are good leader, but because you are honest and fair. They can be considered lazy and will only do what is required of them. So again, you need to know your followers. You will need to learn what it takes to get the most out of them, what will motivate them. These followers will probably require more of your time to insure they complete their task. Sometimes, it is how you use them within your team. It may only take putting them working with the right teammate.

I know you thinking, just get rid of them. Let them go, and get better people. Sometimes, that is your only option. But remember, the next person may be worse or not able to do what you need done if you can't find another employee.

Good leaders can make the best with what they have. Remember knowing their strengths, weaknesses, and behaviors, you can manipulate them into doing their task as required.

This covers most of the basic things. You, as leaders, probably already do a lot that we have discussed. This is because it comes naturally to you. The inherent leadership trait has already become dominant for you. So, this means you are on the right path.

I going to give you some tools to use, some behavior to watch for, to help you to become even a better leader.

With all the different styles, when you use the tools, you will be using what I like to think of as a method Like I to call **"Suggestive leader"**.

The Suggestive leader uses a person's behaviors, personality, and desires to accomplish common goals and helps to develop or enhance the individual's own natural abilities. You can do this in subtle ways, as you will see.

CHAPTER 4

SUBCONSCIOUS AND WORDS

I've talked about the research done on genetic traits that relate to leadership and followers and how there is a collation to each other.

Knowing this exists is to show you that you have common ground with your followers and how it helps in achieving your goals, however, without having some knowledge of the psychology of your subconscious and how the uses of words can create immediate emotions, it would be hard to put all this into practical use.

There was a study done by Stanford University in 1998 that showed how the use of certain words creates a positive or a negative reaction in your subconscious. This can affect how a person responds to you or how they feel about you. It also found certain reactions that are common and could be beneficial to you, as a leader.

This study took 240 subjects and tested them in several situations involving instructional dialogue, group discussions, and stressful debate. During these studies, they evaluate how the brain reacted and how the subject felt after tests.

One of the tests was instructional-related. They call subjects in and give them instruction with just the facts and thank them. They then sent them away to do the task.

The second time, they would do the same thing, but this time, they would say the subject's name at least three times during the instruction.

The third time, same as the second, but this time, they told them that we thought with their abilities and the instructor noted they knew they could do the assignment.

During this test, they monitored the subjects' brains active in the frontopolar cortex, medial temporal lobes and the medial parietal cortex (this is the area where they believe the subconscious is). Also, after the instructions, they all questioned them with a series of questions.

Brain activity grew from the first test to the second test, and more on the third test. It showed they were more engaged on the third test, and the pattern also showed to be more positive.

From the questions, on the first test, the subjects felt like they had to do the assignment because they were instructed to do so. They also didn't know if the instructor liked them or not, and they weren't 100 percent sure they could do the assignment. They also felt that their assignment was probably harder than the assignment given to the others. (They didn't know that the assignments were the same for all subjects.)

Things improved on the second test, where they mention the subject name at least three times. They thought the instructor was nice and that he seemed to like them, and they were excited about trying to do the assignment.

The third time, they mentioned the subject's abilities and told them they could handle the assignments. This time, they felt like the instructor liked them and that he has trusted them to do them assignment. They also were sure they would complete the assignment.

This was just one of many the tests they did. It's amazing how just a couple of words can make all the difference in attitudes and emotions. All we need to do is to use positive enforcement in the way we communicate.

Think about it: the uses of their name, talking about their abilities, and the instructor showing confidence in their abilities made all the different. Those three little things turn someone into a follower.

In the remaining chapters, I will show you how to use these and others, along with the natural behaviors.

CHAPTER 5

SUGGESTIVE OR SUBTLE LEADER

Let's face it, most leaders are not the guys who get up and give motivating speeches once a year or the president of a large corporation that you never see. Most of the leaders are the ones tasked with assignments.

It's the supervisors, production managers, project managers, directors, foremen, crew boss, etc. that make up the majority of your leaders. Leaders are the backbone of any company. They are the ones who must find ways to motive their followers every day.

Almost always, they are working with budgets, quotes, schedules, manpower issues, etc. They deal with their own company, owners, vendors, stakeholders, contractors, suppliers, and employees. The Suggestive or Subtle Leader method will be very valuable, because it is something that will be used every day and with almost all they encounter.

This type of leadership is very simple method that anyone can use. This can be used any way and any time, especially in day-to-day operations. It's like being a leader from an equal perspective with your followers. When you use this method, you will be engaging your followers and helping them make decisions that lead them to your common goals and help develop their own skills.

You are going to play off their inherent abilities/ behaviors. You are going to use the desire to help, the want to do, and the desire to satisfy. You are also going to play on their own leadership abilities to influence, control, and manipulate them in getting the job done in a positive, productive way that benefits everyone involved.

Think about this. Most of you will be leading people who get paid by the hour or commission from a product made or sold. For most of them, that is their motivation. Doing the job and getting paid. Most want to do a good job and make you happy. That's that inherent behavior we talk about. But otherwise, they don't have the goals you have. So how can you motive them to follow and reach your goals?

Well, sometimes you don't. What you do is motive them to do their job to the best of their ability. It will be up to you to use their abilities and their goals to reach your goal. Does this make sense?

Let's say we have a product line that makes alarms. This product line needs to produce 100 alarms every four hours to reach your goal. The company requirement is only 90 in four hours. You know it possible, because your team has done it several times and even more. One of the steps is the electrical wiring, and it is the most time-consuming. This step can make the difference in you making your goal or not. This employee is paid by the hour. How do you motivate them to ensure he gets at least the minimum 100 in four hours when he knows the company requirements?

The first thing is to make sure he and the rest of the team knows what your goal is and the reason behind the goal. Whether it's to have the best product line in the company or because you want to prove to the company that the company requirements are too low or whatever.

Second, you want to explain that they are the best and that you know they can do this. When they do this, then everyone in the company will know they are the best, and they should be proud of what they do. You want them to know this is a team effort and each step is important.

Now, you would tell them you need their help. They need to let you know if there is anything that needs to be done to achieve this goal. Let them know they are the experts and you trust their judgement. Also, ask if there is anything you can do to help them to be more productive.

And last, if possible, speak to each follower and express your confidence in them, including the guy who does the electrical. Sometimes, you have too many followers to do this, and you will still need to talk to the key players, including the electrical step people.

This is more of the real world and the day-to-day problems you deal with. That's why the Suggestive leader will be beneficial to you. What did I communicate to my followers?

1. I gave them the goal – the vision.
2. I gave them the reason – honest.
3. I know they are the best - built confidence.
4. I let them know I was proud - everyone will know – motivation.
5. I asked for their help – you showed you trust them.
6. We are a team, each one as important as the other – bonding.
7. When possible, speak to each one – personal.
8. I also gave them control, but didn't give up control, either. They know it's up to them; they own it.

This example is can be played out in many different situations. It's really a simple way to communicate. You probably already do this sometimes. But you need to learn to do this all the time. Be consistent all the time. You, as a leader, need to be prepared to address problems, give directions, build confidence, and motivate your followers at any given time. Being consistent helps build trust and respect from all you interact with.

1. Use their name several times during conversation.
2. Give good instructions.
3. Mention their abilities.
4. Show you have confidence in them.

Very simple things that are **positive** to the subconscious. Easy to use.

CHAPTER 6

GOOD LEADERS

Good leaders come in all sizes and shapes. But to be good at what you do, some things are needed. A leader must be:

- **In a position of influence or in authority.**
- **An expert or have good general knowledge.**
- **Know the facts as they exist.**
- **Have an investment.**

- **Honest.**
- **Compassionate.**
- **Knowledgeable about their followers.**
- **A good communicator.**

Most leaders are some type of supervisor, and their followers are paid employees. But the concept of leadership is still the same.

Most leaders only lead about eight to 20 employees directly. You may have others who are under you in an indirect way that you interact with from time to time, but they usually have a leader/supervisor/foreman who works for you and is a direct follower of yours.

Your followers, as I mentioned, may be leaders themselves and need the same things you do. But they still need a mentor. I mention this, because sometimes, how you give directions to your followers will be passed down to their followers. So, good communication is a must.

Okay, let's look at the requirements one by one:

In a position of influence or in authority: can be anyone who has followers. Like a journeyman and his helpers or a senior programmer and his assistants. Could be a foreman and his crew or project manager and his team. A lawyer and his interns. In other words, it could be almost anyone.

Know the facts as they exist: being informed of the situation is very important. We never want to be the blind leading the blind. You must have a good general knowledge of the task at hand and be current with the progress.

During my training classes, I tell the story of being stopped by a police officer for speeding in a small town in La. The officer asked for me to get out of the car and come to the back of the car after he told me he pulled me over for speeding. As I got out of the car, I noticed the back of a speed sign about 100 yards behind me.

I decided that I would try and "take control" and talk myself out of a ticket. As I stepped up next to the officer, I said, "Officer Daniel, I noticed the speed limit sign, and I was starting to slow down." I pointed at the sign. "I really was slowing down. You think maybe you could do me a little favor and just give me as warning this time?" I asked the officer.

I spoke first, called him by his name, asked for a little favor, pointed at the sign, showing I was knowledgeable about the speed. I had taken control— well, at least I thought I had.

Then, Officer Daniel said, "Mr. Collins, if you look hard, you will see another one of the speed signs about 300 yards before this sign, and if you could see farther down the road another 300 to 400 yards, you would see another speed limit sign."

"Mr. Collins," he said, "if you would have slowed down after the first sign, I wouldn't even have pulled you over. If you would have slowed down after the second sign, I might have pulled you over and probably given you a warning. But Mr. Collins, when pass this third sign and are still speeding, you are going to receive a ticket, a speeding violation, which you can pay or go the court and plea your case to the judge. I highly suggest your pay your ticket."

So, the moral of this story is first, don't speed, and the second, know all the facts. It hard to lead (that control) without the facts.

Have an investment: The leader has a stake in the project. This is the difference from a leader and a motivator. A motivator doesn't have to be invested in your project. He doesn't need to know anything about it. He depends on your inherent behaviors to stimulate you, to make you feel better about yourself. So, you feel like you can do anything for a period of time. That might be his only involvement.

Where a leader has knowledge and has stake in the project, he has a goal or a vision to accomplish. He will lead and motivate his followers to helping to complete the required tasks in a way that it becomes their goal, as well. Day in and day out.

Honest: Always be honest with your followers. Credibility is a must for a leader. This comes from being honest and doing what you say. Your follower will mimic you. If you always hold up your end, the follower will more likely hold up their end. Think for a minute: who do you do you trust? Someone who lies or someone who is honest? You need your followers to trust you.

Let me go a little deeper on this. There will be times that you have things that you don't want to tell your followers or can't. Don't open that door; keep the conversation going in the direction you want it to go. But never lie. There is always a way to avoid it.

There will be times that you may have a problem with one of your followers not meeting expectations. This can be handled honestly, but in a positive way. Remember, you are also helping your follower to improve.

Compassionate: You always hear the term "be compassionate about what you do." What does this mean? The definition of compassion is: pity, sympathy, **caring, concern**, solicitude, sensitivity, **love,** mercy, **tolerance**, kindness, **humanity,** charity, and **leniency**.

A leader should always care about what he does or says. Concern for the people and the project. Love what he does and the end results. Must have tolerance to reach the goal, with his followers and any distractions that might derail the "common goals". Having compassion for your followers involves caring, concern, love, tolerance, humanity, and leniency.

If a leader knows his followers, he will have compassion for them. This emotional trait gives you the follower's habits, behaviors, abilities, and ambitions. Compassion is essential in being a good leader. Without compassion, it would be hard to get anyone to follow you. Don't get compassion confused with weakness. Used correctly, compassion is a strength.

Tolerance is something we don't always think about. We all have levels of tolerance in almost everything we do. What movies we watch, our friends, stores we shop at, our coworkers, our leaders, our followers, etc. Learning about yourself and what tolerance level you have towards failure and success will be useful.

What does failure mean to you? Is it an end result? A stepping stone? Just a direction changer? Learning moment? Knowing what it means to you and how you handle it will reflect on how you lead. If failure stops you, it will stop your followers. I always look at it as an opportunity to show others that it is just a distraction, but doesn't stop you from reaching your final goals or vision.

Success comes in many forms. Of course, it's a success to reach your goal, but how about all the things to get there? They are success also. Success can be as little as getting someone to agree with you, someone completing your instructions, resolving an issue, etc. Your greatest success is how well you lead, minute by minute, hour by hour, day by day, and project to project.

Humanity is defined as: man, people, beings, human's race, mortals, and human nature. So, you must be human, never think of yourself as someone special or different than your followers. The old sayings, "Put your foot in his shoes" or "Walk a mile in his shoes" are things you should always consider when you are leading. Again, knowing your followers will help you to "walk in their shoes".

Leniency is a little tricky. The definition is: the quality of being merciful or tolerant or forgiveness. This goes back to humanity. Never be too quick to judge someone or the act. I think this is where being humble comes into play. Remember, you are a leader all the time. How you handle people is a reflection of you. If you expect respect and compassion, you must have some leniency in dealing with your followers.

Knowledgeable about their followers: knowing your followers. These are the people working directly for you and any you have some contact with. What am I talking about here?

You need to understand their personalities, their abilities, their work behavior, and what's valuable to them. This is easy to do by just visiting with them and discussing several different topics. From work to family and play. Everything they tell you, look at the body language, their eyes. How they express themselves. Where is their compassion? Are they invested? Do they appear honest and trustworthy? Are they knowledgeable? How well do they communicate? Yes. You are looking for the same things that makes a good leader. It also applies to the follower.

A good communicator: I saved this till the last. Not because it's the least important, because it the most important. Being able to communicate is the key to your success. If you encompass all the other traits into your communication, you will be successful. You will be preceded and judged from the way you communicate.

Communication starts with all the items above. Position of influence, being an expert, knowing the facts, being invested, honest, compassionate, and having a relationship with your followers. The next step is the delivery. How you give the message to your followers. You must make sure you are communicating in a way they understand, and that the goal is clear. Now, this is harder than it sounds. Details, details are so important!

During my training, I give everyone an assignment as follows:

A small boy of four or five is sitting at the kitchen table with his dad. The little boy says, "Dad, I want to get my own glass of water by myself to drink while I eat my snack." The dad thinks for a couple minutes, looks at the counter, sink, and cabinet. The table is only a few feet from the sink. He knows his son can reach the top of the counter, but can't reach the faucet or the cabinet. The boy's plastic cup is in the cabinet next to the sink. Then, the dad thinks to himself, "There is a way for him to do it." Then, he says to his son, "Okay, I will let you get a drink of water by yourself, but you must do what I tell you to do, okay?" The little boy agrees, and the dad starts with his instructions.

Now, you are the Dad. Write out the instructions you are going to give to this little boy, so he can get a drink of water by himself.

Remember he is only four or five years old.

???

So, how you do? Did you give good instructions in a way the little boy could understand? Did you consider all the elements to accomplish the task? Did you do it in an encouraging way? Did you leave out any steps to complete the task?

Okay, here is the way it should go:

"Son, do you know what the counter is?" As he walks over and puts his hand on the counter. The young boy nods his head, yes. "Okay, show me where you cup is?" The dad asks. The little boy gets up and points at the cabinet, where his cup is.

Okay, good. I'm going to tell you what to do as you do it. We will finish one thing at a time, then I will tell you what to do next.

I want you to slide your chair next to the counter at the cabinet where your cup is. Make sure the chair is next to the counter. Then, you climb on the chair, hold on to the back of the chair with one hand, then open the cabinet door with the other hand. Then, reach inside and grab your cup. Set it down on the counter right next to the sink. Good.

Then, close the cabinet door. Crawl down off the chair carefully, so you don't fall. Then, push the chair over in front of the sink. Keep the chair close to the counter. Okay, climb back on the chair, and hold the back of the chair, so you don't fall.

Then, reach out and turn the faucet to the right, towards the cabinet, to turn on the cold water. With that done, now with the same hand, reach over and get your cup and fill it up with water. Not too much, where it is running out you cup. Now, set your cup down on the counter, close to the front of the counter. Now, reach back and turn the water off.

Once you have done this, you need to crawl off the chair carefully. Slide the chair back to the table. Then, go and get your cup off the counter and bring it to the table, walking slowly, so you don't spill it and set it beside your snack. Good job!!

So, how did you really do???

I left one detail out on purpose. What detail did I leave out? Remember, I'm talking to a four or five-year-old. We may use language he doesn't understand or what item did I leave out. Do you think he knows what a faucet is??? Did I ask him? No, I didn't.

This is a simple example of using good communications to accomplish a task. Be sure and talk in a way that is easy to understand. Sometimes, we assume everyone understands what you say. But the truth is, we talk over their heads, or we don't give enough detail for them to follow a lot of times. Big words are not always necessary—never assume they know what you are talking about. Be detailed with your instructions. Think about it. How many times has someone said to you, "I didn't know that's what you meant or if that's what you wanted?" **Poor communication is our fault, not the follower's.**

Just because you have three degrees and one is in English and literature and you have a very large vocabulary, doesn't always help you communicate. **You must communicate on the follower's level, not yours.**

CHAPTER 7

TO INFLUENCE OR TO FOLLOW SOMEONE

Leaders lead and Followers follow. What makes it work? In the workplace, there are always two or three things the leader and follower have in common. The project, both are invested, usually they know what the reward is. This helps you as a leader.

Here are some things that make it work:

Must have a common goal. These goals are normally simple. There may be a project to complete. Or working towards a deadline. Reaching a certain production goal. Normally, you and the team are all there to complete a task, whatever it may be. You just need make sure everyone understands the goal and how you are going to get there.

An investment. All have a stake in what you are doing. Responsible for the results. Basically, you all are committed to the task. For some of your followers, their stake may just be doing their job and earning their paycheck. Note I said earned. They know they must have the job to get the check and to keep the job they know they must follow their leader's instructions to the best of their abilities, so the goal can be reached.

Some type of reward. This may be as simple as completing the task or knowing you can move on to something new. Recognition may be your reward. In some cases, there are monetary benefits. The satisfaction of completing the task under budget and on time is award enough. It is important to know what the rewards are. In a lot of the cases, completing the task means you keep your job. It's just that simple.

So, why is this important? You can't lead if you don't have followers. If they are not in tune with the goal, they can't do the best job. If they are not invested in the task, they won't see the reward and again, they won't perform as they should. If you fail in your directions or establishing your goal and not communicating the rewards, then they can't complete the task.

A followable direction and possible. A followable direction is a giving. Good communication is the key here. Make sure they understand the task/ goal and what it takes to get there. Even when thinking outside the box. The goal has to be achievable. If the followers can't see the possibility, they're not going to follow you.

Just like going to Mars. They have to think outside the box. We know we can send a ship there; we've done that. We know what it takes live in space for long periods of time. We've done that on the space lab. But details like how to carry enough food, water, and fuel to make the trip and the return trip, all these still must be resolved, but the goal of going to Mars is possible. A real vision.

Know the penalties for not completing the task/goal. There is always some type of consequences for not completing a goal or task. Sometimes, it might mean you have to do it again, or extend the time to get it done. Could be a dissatisfied customer or a true failure. But in some cases, it can have financial cost or loss in employment. Whatever it may be, transparency is important when leading your followers.

As a leader, you want to influence your followers to buy in to your plan and to carry out the task to the best of their abilities because they want to. They must know the vision, what it takes to reach that goal, and what happens if the team doesn't make the goal. How you influence them is with communication, as discussed earlier. With good knowledge, compassion, commitment/ investment, be honest, and in a way they understand.

I know some of you are thinking, *I'm not a good speaker or motivator. How do I deliver my message/ directions and make them want to do it?* If you talk about the task with what I said above and you know your followers, you will communicate you message, and they will follow. Remember, they already want to help you; just lead the way.

Also, there are tools to use to help you with your communication. We are going to spend some time on them. They will make your day-to-day leadership easier if you use them.

But before we move on, there are some things that leaders should never do.

Never ask for big favors. The "big" throws out a negative. They will automatically wonder if they can do the favor before you tell them what it is. Asking for a little favor is positive and subconsciously make them feel that you like them and you trust them. Funny, how one word can make such a difference.

Never demand results. Demanding makes the follower feel you don't like them, and they will subconsciously resent you for it. In some businesses, pressure to complete an assignment is great. Don't let yourself reach a point you think you have to demand results to get the job done. If you reach this point, it means you failed somewhere down the road. This negative impact will make followers less productive, and you may lose followers.

Never dismiss someone's solution/answer/opinion until you have all the facts. If you do and for some reason the facts shows their answer was a reasonable solution, subconsciously, they will feel you degraded them, and they will lose some respect for you. They will also think their opinion doesn't matter. Apologizing will help, but it may not heal the wound.

Never be too proud to acknowledge when you are wrong. To acknowledge it makes you human or just like them. Subconsciously, they will like you more. Admitting you were wrong also shows you are honest and will be responsible for your actions. You don't blame others for your mistake.

Never think you can't be part of a problem. Sometimes, leaders forget they are part of the team. And when we don't do our job—whether it's not giving good instructions or a clear vision—then, we are the problem. Maybe we need to get more informed, or maybe we set goals too high to reach. We need to always be evaluating our actions and not letting the team down.

Never let your emotions take over. Sometimes, this is easier said than done. But if you do, you lose control as a leader. It's not that we don't have emotions, we are going to get upset or mad from time to time. But when we act, we must act with our good judgement and in a civil manner. If we lose control of our emotions and fly off the handle, we are causing more damage than good. Also, if we can't control our emotions, others will wonder what else we can't control. Always be professional. If you are angry, step back and think before you speak.

CHAPTER 8

LEADERS' BEHAVIORS

Leadership is not about titles, positions or flowcharts. It is about one life influencing another.

John C. Maxwell

The behavior of a leader should always be to improve communication and relationships with your followers and associates. I mention associates, which could be other leaders, customers, owners, or maybe your boss, because how you relate to these people could affect you followers.

Dale Carnegie says, "There are four ways, and only four ways, in which we have contact with the world. We are evaluated and classified by these four contacts:

1. What we do,

2. How we look,

3. What we say, and

4. How we say it."

This is still true today. It doesn't matter if it is in person, by letter, by phone, by text, or by email. This is why your behavior is most important. Again, you are a leader. Leadership is a full-time job.

The following behaviors can be used with several different types of leadership styles, and they go well with the "Suggestive Leader".

So, let's look at some behaviors that will benefit you.

1. **Respect is always important:** Not just to you, but to all who you deal with. Respecting others demands respect for you. Earning respect is done by being honest, having knowledge, the way you communicate with others, and the way you handle a crisis. You don't have to do anything special, just be a good leader. I want to note that these are the things people look at that might cause them to lose respect for you.

2. **Introductions:** Always greet people positively, with good eye contact, good grip if you shake hands, and to show respect, repeat their name—at least once—after they have said it to you.

When I talk about being positive, it means with a smile and stepping toward them.

Making eye contact not only shows respect, but it also shows you are confident. Also, by looking them in the eyes and repeating their name subconsciously makes them feel good and also makes them think you like them.

3. **Communication:** When you are giving instructions or just visiting, it must be a two-way conversation. Engaging the other party, whether it's just feedback, answering questions, or asking for their opinion is important. It engages their mind on the topic at hand, gets their attention, and it makes it personal. If giving instructions, it is a way to tell if they understand.

4. **Small talk:** Telling a little about yourself, no matter how small or detailed, it makes the followers feel like you are human and you like them, which makes them want to do things for you. Remember what Nick Boothman said about storytelling. Maybe a story would be good.

5. **Small/little favors:** Asking for small/little favors subconsciously makes them think you like them and trust them. Remember what I said about the big favors? They are a negative; not like little favors.

   There are several ways to ask for little favors. Do you mind doing a little something for me? Since you have a relationship with (whoever), would you stop and talk to them about…? You don't necessarily need to use the word "favor".

6. **Your team is an extension of you:** Always remember that team is one. From the worst to the best. Always one. So, never talk bad about one of your team members to another team member. I know there are times that a discussion about one of the team members may be necessary, but how you handle it is very important for you and the team members. Or you might need to address a problem with a team member. You can be positive and still cover the issues that need to be addressed.

   Here an example: Say you have one of your team members that has started showing up late and/or has missed few days. Now you need to address this before it gets out of hand, and other team members complain or dislike you, because you haven't addressed it. For the example, we will call him David.

"David, before you start working on your assignment, I need to discuss something with you. Come on to my office, and we will talk there." Start walking -taking control. Once he in the office, ask him to sit down and close the door. You sit down as well. Then you say, "David, I noticed you have been late/ missing work. Is something going on I need to know about or something I can help with?" Personally concerned.

At this point, he may give you a good reason like: "My wife's job has started requiring her to be out of town some, and we haven't set up any daycare to help with this, but we plan to. I have been filling in the gaps with regular daycare."

Remember compassion. "Well, David I understand things like this happen. Do you need couple days off to get something lined up or is this just temporary?" You show you care, offered help. "You know you are an important part of our team, and when you are late or don't show without our prior knowledge, then we have to make some unplanned adjustments to cover your area. You being here is important to the team. You tell me, what we, the team, can do to help." You showed they are important to you.

Now, at this point he is going to accept your offer of time off to get something setup, or he going to tell you no, that he and his wife should have it figured out in a couple days. At this point is where you have the opportunity to reinforce your requirements. "Okay, David, I hope so. You understand the importance of you being here, on time and every day? We need you." He will probably say yes. "Good, I can count on you and I don't have to worry about having another conversation about this, correct?" You showed trust. He's probably going to agree. "David, you know if you need to be off work, let me know in advance, and I can make plans with the rest of the team to cover your area without any disruptions. Okay?" He will say, "Okay."

"David, one last thing—I'm going to make a note about why you have been late/off work, so others will know and that we had this discussion. I'll put it in your personnel folder for your benefit and mine."

Now as a leader, you took control, kept it private, which shows respect, you showed compassion, caring, trust, and let him know he is important to the team. At the same time, you noted he had a problem, reinforced the requirements, let him know the expectation, let him know it wouldn't be good to have this happen again and that there is a record of this. Also, did you notice I continued to use his name? What does this mean? It helped, because it's positive. It helps making him feel good and that I like him.

Again, this is just an example. Every situation will be different, but can basically be handled in a similar way.

7. **If something is new, teach it:** You have a new assignment. You have acquired some new knowledge with this assignment. Sharing this knowledge will not only help you remember what you learned, but help develop your team. Teaching someone to do their assignment or knowledge to help them be better at their assignment is a win / win situation. It shows you care.

   Just a note: Sometimes when you teach, if we are not careful, the follower will think you are wanting to do the assignment and let you do it. Don't get caught in this trap.

8. **Habit of being accessible:** Depending on what your position is and what your job is, if you always make yourself accessible to your followers, it makes you part of the team and shows you want them to come to you if help is needed. They will make more effort in keeping you informed.

   If you have an office, there are times you may need the door closed. But when possible, have the door open. Also, when possible, always make a point of talking with each of your followers daily. Even if it just small talk. Again, this shows you like them, and you are building trust. I know this may be hard to do if you have several people under you or in different locations, but do the best you can.

9. **Let your followers do their jobs:** What does this mean? If you are doing your job as a leader and trying to develop your follower

abilities, give them good instruction and let them complete the task in their way. This doesn't mean total hands off. But give them room to do it their way. Sometimes, it may be the same way you would do something, but other times it may not. That's not a bad thing. You are helping them build confidence in their abilities and their way may be better than yours.

I know from my own experience in the past when I first became a supervisor, I wanted to show everyone my way and would sometimes stop them in the middle of an assignment and tell them how I would do it. Then, I realized my way wasn't always the best, and I started noticing my followers would resent me in doing it. I was also making them feel as if I didn't trust their judgement.

Remember communication is a two-way street. Give them instructions, discuss it with them to be sure they understand, and turn them loose to do the job. Yes, there's going to be mistakes, but they will be far in-between if you are doing your job.

10. **Give credit where credit is due:** You, being the leader, may get recognized on a job well done, and will probably be desiring, because you are the team leader, but don't forget that the team desires the credit, too. If this happens, let the team know. If it's because of something one of your team members did, be sure they get the credit. Recognize them in a group meeting. This is always positive and shows you appreciate them.

11. **Appearance:** Appearance matters. Being a leader is a full-time job. How you appear to others gives them the first impression of you. If you are a leader, you need to look like a leader. What does a leader look like? That depends on the Industry you work in and what is acceptable attire.

We know that a principle of a law firm will dress differently than a construction supervisor, and the supervisor will dress different than a head chef of a fine restaurant. However, they are all leaders.

The point is, the way you dress tell everyone a little about you. Think about it. If you to dress a little sloppy, then the impression is, you are a sloppy person. If you overdress, then the impression is that you may have a tendency to exaggerate. If you dress in a way that not proper for the industry you are in, it may leave an impression that you may not be very knowledgeable about the industry.

I have a rule to follow. Dress as if you were interviewing for a supervisor's position in whatever industry you work in. This may not be a surefire way to dress, but it is a good starting point. So, get in the habit of dressing as a leader.

12. **Planning:** Always planning. Now, you may have a project plan, three-week look-a-head, a delivery schedule, etc. that you help formulate and keep current. They will tell you the steps to get from A to Z.

But that's is a small part of day-to-day leadership. You will always be planning what you can do to make things better and for the what ifs. Getting from A to Z is always easy on paper. Just follow the alphabet. However, it's never that easy. You need to plan how your followers can keep you on track. Your followers are your manpower. Who goes where? Who can do the best here? Who has this ability? How do I motivate them? Always looking for the best avenue to achieve your goal.

CHAPTER 9

LEADERSHIP TOOLS

I call these tools because they can help you communicate better, understand others better, and could give you the upper hand in a discussion or a debate.

Some of these I may have already used in some of the examples I used before in previous chapters, but it is worth repeating again.

Taking control/never taking control: This is about leading your followers in a way they feel they are part of making the plan. The more involved they are, they more they own the task. By using keywords, two-way communication, asking suggestions or opinions, and having them confirm they understand the instructions, they will feel they have control of their assignment. Which they do, but you lead them that direction. Again, it helps develop you employees and gets more of a commitment for them.

Questions for directions: By asking questions will put the follower's brain in forward motion. This will help get his attend, focused on the assignment and thinking about what needs to be done to reach the goal. Questions like: Have you thought about the material you need? Or maybe, how many employees you need to complete the task? Did you do a mini-schedule?

These types of questions let them start taking control of the activity. He starts to own the assignment. In a sense, you are letting them lead themselves with your guidance.

Buildups: We talked about how important it is to have confidence. Talking about their abilities and the confidence you have in them to carry out their assignments will give them more confidence. This can be as easy as saying things like: "With your abilities, this is right up your alley," or "This is something I know you can do with your abilities," or "I know you can handle this."

This create positive waves in the subconscious and makes the person feel like he can do what's required. Remember this also makes them feel you like and trust them.

Names/ recognition: I mention about saying a person's name when introduced. If you continue to use their name at least three more times during conversation or instructions, they will feel like you like them. It also causes positive waves to the subconscious and builds their confidence. Remember, the more someone likes you, the more they will want to do for you. The inherent behavior to help gets stronger.

Games/ all win: You will have some followers very competitive, and you may handle these people by playing a simple game of "I challenge you". Make them want to prove you wrong. Maybe you give them the assignment that is scheduled for four days and you ask what they think. They come back by saying, "I can do this in three days." Then you reply, 'I have total confidence in you, but there's no way this can be done in three days". Then, the challenge is on, and that's all the motivation they need.

Motivation/satisfaction: In the real world, motivation isn't always the same for each person. Yes, there is a common goal to reach, and it is a motivation in itself. But it still takes more to get the most out of your followers. Using the inherent behavior of want to help and to satisfy you, you can build on these and motivate them by building their confidence. The more you show you have confidence in them, the more they will want to satisfy you. This will be their motivation. Remember, I told you, sometimes, you have to help them reach their goal to reach your goal.

Help me /I don't know: Sometimes, the best way to lead is to let them tell you what they are going to do. Prompting them to give you the information needed to complete the assignment. Just saying the simple statement, "I need help with this," can lead to them telling you how they think it needs to be done. This gets them involved. It creates ownership and helps develop the followers. This is similar to not taking control, but from a different direction.

Interaction is so important for a successful leader/ follower relationship. There will always be times they will look to you for direction and leadership. By having them involved as much as possible builds respect for you and makes them want to follow you even more.

Even table / never standup: When possible, if you need to discuss something that is important with your follower/ followers, sit down. Doing this first signals that this is important, and if you all are at the same level eye contact wise. It helps get their attention and builds trust. If you must stand, do it in a form of a circle; this expresses a connection with all parties. It reinforces the team atmosphere.

Directions /Speaking: If you ever watch good speakers, they never speak too fast. They almost always pause from time to time. A lot of them have sort of a rhythm to their speech. This isn't by accident. Have a little rhythm as you speak translates to the brain as music and is a positive brain wave. Not speaking too fast helps the listener to process the information, and the pause allows the subconscious to form an opinion for the information.

This isn't just me saying this. There have been research projects done on this subject.

This applies to everyday leadership. Never be in a hurry in giving instructions or answering a question. Take your time, allow for the follower to process the information. Again, good communication is so important.

Silent / yes or no: Sometimes after giving instructions or stating a fact, be silent. This will make other feel they need to say something or encourage others to speak, ask questions or give comments, which could lead to a beneficial discussion. The same applies to simple yes or no answer. When you don't elaborate on your answer, it makes others want to know more about your answer.

This also works well in meeting where a debate has broken out about a subject and has stalled. This can get it moving again with more input. Also, if someone gives you an unsatisfactory answer, don't say anything, wait, and they will elaborate more details of the answer.

Remember, good communication is a two-way street. In all these suggestions, you are doing it in a positive way. The subconscious mind functions better with positive waves.

CHAPTER 10

OTHER BENEFICIAL INFORMATION

Here's a few more thing for leaders to consider.

Awareness: There is a difference between management and employees, bosses and workers. Good leaders understand the nature of this difference and accept it. They conduct themselves in a way that sets them apart from their employees—not in a manner that suggests they are better than them, but in a way that permits them to retain an objective perspective with everything that's going on within their control.

Decisiveness: All leaders must make tough decisions._ It goes with the job. They understand that in certain situations, difficult and timely decisions must be made in the best interests of the entire organization, decisions that require a firmness, authority, and finality. Leaders don't hesitate in such situations. They also know when not to act unilaterally, but instead, foster collaborative decision-making. They make every effort in keeping their decision producing positive results.

Confidence: Not only are the best leaders confident, but their confidence is contagious. Employees are naturally drawn to them, seek their advice, and feel more confident as a result. When challenged, they don't give in too easily, because they know their ideas, opinions, and strategies are well-informed and the result of much hard work. But when proven wrong, they take responsibility and quickly act to improve the situations within the authority.

Optimism: The very best leaders are a source of positive energy. They communicate easily. They are helpful and genuinely concerned for other people's welfare. They always seem to have a solution, and always know what to say to inspire and reassure. They avoid negativity and look for ways to get people to work together efficiently and effectively as a team.

Focus: Extraordinary leaders plan ahead. They think through multiple scenarios and the possible impacts of their decisions, while considering alternatives and making plans and strategies—all targeted toward success. Once prepared, they communicate their plans to key players and have contingency plans in the event that last-minute changes require a new direction (which they often do).

Inspiration: Put it all together, good leaders are someone who communicates clearly, concisely, and often, and by doing so motivates everyone to give his or her best all the time. They challenge their people by setting high but attainable goals, and then giving them the support, tools, training, and latitude to pursue those goals and become the best employees they can possibly be.

Some other things that came out of the research: A list of observations that should help you with work, rest, and play with more confidence.

1. During an introduction, make a note of someone's eye color. You're not going to use the information (unless you plan to write them a poem) – it's just a technique to achieve the optimum amount of eye contact, which people find friendly and confident.

2. People always have the clearest memory of the first and last thing that happens, while the middle becomes a vague blur. So, as a

leader, you want to ask if your instructions are clear or ask for them to repeat them. If you bring up something in the middle of a meeting, you might want to repeat it the end of the meeting during recap period. If you're setting the time for an interview, try and be the first or last through the door.

3. People's feet are often an insight into what they're thinking. For example, if you approach two people talking and they turn their torso to you but not their feet, they'd prefer you left them alone. Similarly, if you're talking to someone and their feet are pointing away from you, they want to escape.

4. When laughter breaks out in a group of people, each one will instinctively glance at whichever other individual they feel closest to in that group. Might be a way to see who your allies are or who your enemies are. (This is also a good way of spotting who is secretly sleeping together at work.)

5. Like all therapists worth their fee, remember to use the power of silence. If someone gives you an unsatisfactory answer to a question, stay quiet and keep eye contact, and they'll usually feel pressured to keep talking and reveal more.

6. If you know someone is going to have a go at you in a meeting, deliberately sit right next to them. The proximity and mirrored direction of your bodies will make them feel less comfortable with being aggressive, and you'll have an easier time of it.

7. Mirroring people's body language when you interact with them is a way of building up trust. Just be subtle about it.

8. When walking through a crowd, keep your gaze on the gaps between people rather than the people themselves. Usually, they'll part ways to let you through, meaning less *West Side Story* moments on Oxford Street.

9. A date that involves adrenalin – rollercoasters, horror films, etc. – will help simulate arousal in the brain, and make people think they're enjoying your company. Which hopefully they will be anyway.

10. A warm handshake makes you far more attractive to people than a cold one. The lesson here? Invest in some gloves.

11. The best way to learn is to teach. If you're acquiring a new skill or piece of knowledge, bore someone else with it at the first opportunity you get.

12. Finally: there is nothing more important to people than their self-image. Figure out how people like to think of themselves, and challenge or reinforce it to your advantage.

As with all of these, please use responsibly.

CHAPTER 11

THE WRAP UP

When we think about leaders, we think about people who are in the photos in the book. We can all remember something about what made them great leaders.

But as great of leaders as they are, also of leaders of other leaders that took care of the daily activities. I don't want to take anything away from these people, because they are great leaders and inspired many people during their time. Even today, we still use their quotes, follow their styles, and mention them all the time in connection with motivators, leaders, and inspirers.

What I want to say, don't think your role as a leader is anything less than theirs. Someday, one of you may be considered among these leaders. But most of you will never have your name in the lights. But being the leader of a company, school, business, crew, project, etc., your responsibilities are just as important.

As leaders, you are there to make a difference, to influence the outcome of whatever the project is and of the people around you. If you inspire one person or motivate someone to do more or help develop a new leader and made your company look good. You are a good leader that many will look up to and respect for days to come.

What you have learned here is that "You are a natural leader." As you grow, you will develop your own style of leadership. One style isn't any better than another, but how you communicate is the key to how successful you are. I hope I have given you some tool to use in communicating.

This book is a guide for you to use in your development and ways to communicate using the simple knowledge of human behavior. Study after study shows us that positive people are more productive than negative people. The more we can reinforce positive things for the subconscious, the more you will influence others to do things for you and because they want to.

There isn't a better feeling than to know you influenced at team of people to accomplish a largescale vision or goal. It is only possible by building a team of followers, giving a clear picture of the goal, giving all the tools they need, and supporting them along the way.

My goal with this book was to give everyone at least one or two things that would help them be a better leader and to convey to you that a leader is a full-time job. Leaders don't shut down when they go home; it's a lifestyle. A behavior that you develop as you grow. Good leaders never stop being leaders.

I hope I have reached my goal with you. If so, please teach it to others. The more good leaders we have, the better our world will be.

I have also attached some of my training PowerPoint slides, so you will have a quick reference to information within.

I want to finish up by repeating something that Dale Carnegie said that I think is so important for you leaders.

As you read this, think about your leaders or people who inspire you and why they do. Could it be because of the how they manage the items listed below?

Dale Carnegie says, "There are four ways, and only four ways, in which we have contact with the world. We are evaluated and classified by these four contacts:

1. What we do,
2. How we look,
3. What we say, and
4. How we say it."

Thank you,

C. Ray Collins

PRESENTATION INFORMATION

Leadership

- **Democratic:** Places high value on diverse skills, qualities & knowledge base of a team. Ex; Senators
- **Visionary:** Ability to come up with new directions & new potential solutions to a problem. Thinking outside the box. Ex: Steve Jobs
- **Coaching:** One who spends time & energy on individuals in any given group. They will direct, guide & cultivate others based on what influences their desires in a positive way. Ex: Supt and PMs

- **Affiliative:** Places high emphasis on "Team". Building trust within a group & creating emotional bond. A sense of belonging. Praise & Encouragement are important. Ex: Football Coach
- **Pacesetting:** Leads by example. They set and live by high standards & hope others will follow. Ex: Drill Sargent
- **Commanding:** Do as I say because I'm the boss. Gives directives & expect other to follow. Ex: Military Officer

LEADERSHIP:

- The Leader is the "Influencer" "The Controllers"
- The Follower is the "Desire to Help" "Want To"

- These are **inherent abilities** we are all born with!
- Its part of your **natural behavior.**
- You possess both, the "Influencer and the Desire to Help" behavior.
- With other learned behaviors, the Leader and the Follower are very Similar.
- **These similarities are necessary to have a relationship between leader and follower.**

LEADERS

Communicator	Model
Motivator	Fact Finder
Decision Maker	Influencer
Inspirer	Controller
Coach	Problem Solver
Invested	Manipulator
Team Player	Teacher
Negotiator	Honest
Expert	Mentor

FOLLOWERS:

Communicator	Model
Motivator	Fact Finder
Loyal	Submissive
Desire to Help	A Doer
Coachable	Creative
Invested	The Want To
To Belong	Student
Supporter	Loyalty
Expert	

SUGGESTIVE LEADER:

Along with the 6 Types of leaders, there is a leader method that works well with our natural behaviors.

I like to call this the "Suggestive Leader".

This method uses a person behaviors, personality and desires to accomplish common goals and help develop or enhance the individual's own natural abilities.

A Suggestive leader uses Tools of the Trade.

TO INFLUENCE SOMEONE OR TO FOLLOW:

- Common Goal,

- An Investment

- Some type of Award

- A Followable Direction, must be possible.

- A Penalty for Not completing the Task

GOOD LEADERS:

- Position of influence or Authority
- Expert or good general Knowledge
- Know the Facts
- Investment
- Compassion
- Honest
- Know the Followers

LEADERSHIP DON'TS:

Never ask for a big favor

Never demand results

Never dismiss someone's solution until you have all the facts

Never be too proud to acknowledge when you were wrong

Never think you can't be part of the problem or failure

Never let your emotions take over

TOOLS FOR THE SUGGESTIVE LEADERS:

- 1. **Take control:** never take control
    Suggestive or Subtle -
- 2. **Question:** for direction
    Asking questions, put the follower brain in forward
- 3. **Buildups:** acknowledge abilities
    Let them know you are asking them to do this because of their ablity. You're the right person for this assignment
- 4. **Names:** Recognition, recognition
    Not only is it charming, but helps build their self esteem and feel special
- 5. **Games: All** winners
    Playing games where you challenge someone or compare something to the activity you want done. Makes them want to prove you wrong or show you, they can do it.

- 6. **Motivate: Satisfaction**

    Challenge can come in many forms: We allow 3 days to do this. With your ability, you can do this in 2 days. I don't think you can do this. I know you can do this. I know you can find a way.

- 7. **I don't know:** the help

    Some time the best way to lead, is to let them lead with prompts

- 8 **Even table:** Never standup

    If this is important, sit down with them. Builds trust.

- 9. Directions/ Speaking: Talk slow, pause from time to time. Let them process the information and form an opinion

- 10. **Silent Yes or No:** sometimes the best discussion

    Sometimes short answers make them think. Remember you help them to help themselves.

ACKNOWLEDGEMENTS, PHOTOS, QUOTES, AND REFERENCES

Photos:

Pg. 3 - 6 Legendary horsemen

Pg. 5 – Tony Robbins – Speaker/Author "Firewalkers Guide to Leadership"

Pg. 10 – Matt Damon and Robin Williams (Movie: *Good Will Hunting*)

Pg. 16 – Group Picture – Unknown

Pg. 19 – Brad Brown – President of Austin Commercial, LP

Pg. 23 – Christopher Andrews – Area Manger Austin Commercial, LP

Pg. 33 – Steve Jobs – Apple; Bill Gates – Microsoft; Charles Branson – Virgin Group

Pg. 55 – Mary Kay – Mary Kay Cosmetics; Gandhi- India Spiritual Leader; John Kennedy – President of USA; Unknown; Steve Jobs – Apple; Martin Luther King – Activist/Minister

Quotes:

Pg. 3 – Vince Lombardi - Coach

Pg. 4 – Dale Carnegie – speaker/author/leader; Dwight Eisenhower – President of the U.S.A.; Randy Stocklin – CEO of One Click Venture; J. Kelly Huey – Author (*Building Your Dream Team*); Nicholas Boothman – author/ speaker/ motivator

Pg. 10 – Andreas Von

Pg. 38 – John Maxwell; Dale Carnegie

Pg. 57 – Dale Carnegie

References only:

Dale Carnegie –*How to Develop Self-Confidence and Influence People by Public Speaking* – first published 1936, last published in 1988

Tony Robbins – "Firewalker's Guide to Leadership" series

Nicholas Boothman – *The Irresistible Power of Story Speak*— published 2017

Harvard University NYU and University of California Research – Genetic Traits – Published 2002

Stanford University – Research – Words and The Subconscious Psychology – Published 1988